Intercessions for the Church Year

A COMPANION TO ASB YEARS 1 & 2

SUSAN SAYERS

Kevin Mayhew

First published in 1991 by
KEVIN MAYHEW LTD
Rattlesden
Bury St Edmunds
Suffolk IP30 0SZ

Intercessions for the Church Year
is extracted from
Springboard to Worship

ISBN 0 86209 169 1

Cover design by Graham Johnstone
Typesetting and Page Creation by Anne Hallam
Printed and bound in Great Britain by
J.B. Offset Printers (Marks Tey) Limited

Contents

Foreword

Surely one of the fundamental duties and joys of being Christians is to bear one another's burdens in prayer, and come in the Spirit of Christ before God our Father, as we plead for the Church and for the world.

Such prayer must involve both the mind and the imagination. To pray effectively we need to stand alongside those for whom we plead. We need to appreciate their hurt and distress, share their anguish, and bring them with us to the healing love of God. The whole church of Christ, praying like this, releases an immense fund of loving power. It enables the creative love of God to renew, energise, restore and bring to wholeness both the Church and the world.

The congregation need to be made aware of the importance of this work in which their participation is so desperately needed by a bewildered and often misguided world. Both the privilege and the responsibility are enormous.

Those who lead the prayer of God's faithful people have the job of creating the best 'climate' for such prayer to take place. Nothing should be rushed; the invitation to pray provides the opportunity to quieten minds and concentrate attention in a receptive stillness. The purpose of each petition is to guide the hearts, minds and imaginations to the point where real pleading, rooted in compassion, can begin. The silences are therefore the culmination of all this preparation, and need to be long enough to allow the people to hold each prayer burden up to the healing and creative presence of God.

The Intercessions I have suggested flow out of the theme for the day and the readings, so that they will be in harmony with the thoughts and ideas already suggested on any particular day.

I suggest that those preparing to lead the Intercessions may find it helpful to base their own words on the petitions provided, altering them, selecting from them or adding to them in whatever way is appropriate for their own particular parish.

These Intercessions are based on those originally published in *Springboard to Worship*, in which the day's theme is explored and developed for all ages and in a variety of ways.

Susan Sayers

9th Sunday before Christmas

God created our universe and everything in it,
including us. He gives us both physical and
spiritual life and sustains his creation with his
constant love. As Lord of life he is worthy of all
the praise, honour and worship that we can offer.

Knowing that when we pray in faith our loving Father
will hear us, let us pray together for the church,
and for the world he has made.

Bless the work of all who spread
the wonderful news of your love.
May all who profess to be Christians
shine with your light so that others are drawn
to know your glory and experience
the joy of your peace.

Pause

Lord our maker: **hear our prayer.**

Sustain and protect Elizabeth our Queen
and guide all world leaders, advisers and politicians
to act with wisdom and integrity.

Pause

Lord our maker: **hear our prayer.**

Father, we commend to your loving keeping
all who have died, especially...

that they may live for ever
in the glorious peace and joy of your heaven.

Pause

Lord our maker: **hear our prayer.**

We offer you thanks and praise
for the rich and beautiful world
you have provided for us,
and for the many blessings in our lives,
and for the gift of life itself.

Pause

Lord our maker: **hear our prayer.**

Merciful Father,
**accept these prayers
for the sake of your Son,
our Saviour Jesus Christ, Amen.**

Almighty God You have created the Heavens & the
earth as Made human beings in Your own
image. Teach us to discern Your hands in all Your
works & to serve You with reverence &
thanksgiving thro Jesus Christ our Lord who with
You & the Holy Spirit reigns supreme over all things
now & for ever.

8th Sunday before Christmas

Sin is destructive. It separates us from God through our disobedience to his will. It was God's love for us that prompted him to give his only Son so that we could be bought back, or redeemed, from the sentence of death and given the chance of new life in Christ.

In the Spirit of Jesus Christ, who can save us from sin, let us pray to our heavenly Father for the Church and for the world.

We pray for all who witness to the truth of saving love, especially those whose Christian witness brings danger, hardship or ridicule.

Pause

Father of Love: **we believe and trust in you.**

We pray for our Queen and all who hold positions of authority in our world; that they may be led to right and just decisions in keeping with your will.

Pause

Father of Love: **we believe and trust in you.**

We pray for the members of our families,
for all those who are precious to us
and those we find difficult to get on with;
strengthen our love for one another
and give us the grace to forgive wholeheartedly.

Pause

Father of Love: **we believe and trust in you.**

We pray for the vulnerable and the frightened,
for those tormented by guilt and those who despair;
give them the comfort of knowing you are with them
and draw them to the light of your forgiveness.

Pause

Father of Love: **we believe and trust in you.**

We pray for those who have died
and for those who mourn;
grant them peace in your presence for ever.

Pause

Father of Love: **we believe and trust in you.**

Thank you, Father, for supplying us always
with the strength we need to do your will,
and for the joy of working with you.
Merciful Father,
accept these prayers
for the sake of your Son
our Saviour Jesus Christ, Amen.

7th Sunday before Christmas

Real faith is bound to be revealed in action.
Abraham was prepared to trust God absolutely,
even when he could not understand what he was
being asked to do, and God honoured such
faith. It is no good talking about having faith in
God if we are not prepared to translate it into
loving action and obedience to his will.

My brothers and sisters in Christ,
bound together in love and faith let us pray for
    the Church and for the world.

O Lord our God, we trust in your promise to hear us
when we pray in faith.

Strengthen us in the certain knowledge
of your constant presence,
so that we witness to your love by the way
we speak and act each day.

Pause

Merciful Father: **hear us as we pray.**

Teach us and guide us to use the resources of the world

wisely and unselfishly, sharing its riches
and respecting its beauty.

Pause

Merciful Father: **hear us as we pray.**

Alert us to the needs of those around us
and increase our friendliness and understanding
in all our relationships.

Pause

Merciful Father: **hear us as we pray.**

Bring your health and wholeness
to those in physical pain and mental anguish,
and give your inner peace
to those overwhelmed with worries.

Pause

Merciful Father: **hear us as we pray.**

Into your hands, Father, we commend
those who have died,
for we know that in your care they are safe.

Pause

Merciful Father: **hear us as we pray.**

And now we want to thank you for your constant love
and kindness, support and protection.

Pause

Merciful Father:
**accept these prayers for the sake of your Son,
our Saviour Jesus Christ, Amen.**

6th Sunday before Christmas

God promises to save his people, and he can be trusted to keep his word. Moses had faith in God's promise to set his people free from slavery. Our faith in Jesus can set us free from the binding chains of sin. He will lead us and protect us from evil.

As children and heirs through adoption,
let us confide in our heavenly Father
who knows us so well.

Father, into your enlightenment and perception
we bring all whose faith is limited by fear or prejudice;
all whose living faith has been replaced
by the empty shell of habit.

Pause

Lord, we believe: **please help our faith to grow.**

Father, into the depths of your wisdom
and understanding we bring those with responsibilities,
and all who have difficult decisions to make;
especially...   and

all in charge of hospitals, schools, factories
and all community services.

Pause
Lord, we believe: **please help our faith to grow.**

Father, into your tireless faithfulness we bring
the members of our families;
any who rely on us for help, support or guidance;
any whom we are being asked to serve
or introduce to your saving love.

Pause
Lord, we believe: **please help our faith to grow.**

Father, into the gentleness of your healing love
we bring all who are in pain;
all those recovering from surgery;
those involved in crippling accidents
or suffering from wasting diseases.

Pause
Lord, we believe: **please help our faith to grow.**

Father, into your lasting peace
we bring all those who have died,
especially...

Pause
Lord, we believe: **please help our faith to grow.**

Father, your character is always
full of mercy and faithfulness;
**accept these prayers for the sake of your Son,
our Saviour Jesus Christ, Amen.**

5th Sunday before Christmas

Through a faithful remnant of God's people, the Good News of God's power and willingness to save is spread to all nations. At every stage of the journey there is bound to be conflict between good and evil, and many will try to lead others astray. But we are to be prepared for this, so that, watchful and alert, we may remain faithful to our calling as followers of Christ.

Companions in Christ
knowing the loyalty and faithfulness
of our Father in Heaven, let us pray to him
for the Church and for our world.

Keep all Christians firm and steadfast in their faith,
with lives that witness clearly
to the power of your love.

Pause

Hear us, Father: **we come to do your will.**

Guide our leaders,
and all those in influential positions,
to uphold and promote Christian values.

Pause

Hear us, Father: **we come to do your will.**

Be present in our homes and our relationships,
and increase our commitment to reconciliation,
encouragement and understanding of one another.

Pause
Hear us, Father: **we come to do your will.**

Give reassurance and peace
to all who are anxious, depressed or confused;
and make us aware of the needs of others.

Pause
Hear us, Father: **we come to do your will.**

Into your safe keeping
we commend all those who have died....
for with you there is eternal life, peace and joy.

Pause
Hear us, Father: **we come to do your will.**

We thank you for all the many blessings
we receive each day,
and in silence we pour out
our individual reasons for gratitude.

Pause
Hear us, Father: **we come to do your will.**

Creator God, Lord of our life,
accept these prayers
for the sake of your Son,
our Saviour Jesus Christ, Amen.

1st Sunday in Advent

We need to prepare ourselves right away so that we shall be ready and receptive when Christ comes again in glory at the end of time. The great hope of Israel has already been fulfilled in the first coming of Jesus, born as a baby. We look back to that with wonder. The enormous love it shows, highlights the supreme goodness and compassion of the God whose second coming we await.

My brothers and sisters in Christ,
as we watch together for his coming
let us pray together for the church and for the world.

Lord, strengthen and guide your church in its mission
to the world; that sinners may be alerted to repentance
and many may be brought to the joy of living
in your love.

Pause

Lord, come to us: **live in us now.**

Lord, we pray for the whole created world
and its peoples; that no evil may thwart your will,
but that rather your kingdom may be established
and your will done.

Pause

Lord, come to us: **live in us now.**

Lord, bless this parish
and all who serve our community;
that we may strive each day to align our lives
with the life of Christ who saves us from sin.

Pause

Lord, come to us: **live in us now.**

Lord, we pray for all who suffer—
mentally, physically and spiritually;
for those who see no further than
immediate, material comforts,
and do not realise their spiritual poverty.

Pause

Lord, come to us: **live in us now.**

We commend to your love
all who have completed their life on earth,
that they may rest in your peace
and share your risen life.

Pause

Lord, come to us: **live in us now.**

Thank you, Lord, for the richness
of your companionship;
for the joy and peace your constant presence gives.

Pause

Lord, come to us: **live in us now.**

Father, we trust in your mercy;
**accept these prayers for the sake of your Son,
our Saviour Jesus Christ, Amen.**

17

2nd Sunday in Advent

God has gradually revealed himself to us through his Word in the Bible. The Old Testament is an unfolding of God's will in creating and leading his people into the way of truth and love. Jesus Christ, in the New Testament, is the fulfilment of all the hopes and prophecies, for in him God lives among his people in person.

As children of our caring, heavenly Father,
let us pray trustfully, now.

Father, inspire all Christians throughout the world
to follow Christ simply and wholeheartedly,
so their lives witness to the beauty
and peace of his kingdom.

Pause

Father of love: **remake our lives.**

May your will be accomplished
through all world leaders, governments
and their advisers;
that they may be enabled to lead their people
wisely and fairly, with understanding and sensitivity.

Pause

Father of love: **remake our lives.**

Father, we bring before you
our own families and loved ones,
especially any from whom we are separated;
that we may learn to see Christ in each face,
and serve him in caring for one another.

Pause

Father of love: **remake our lives.**

We pray for all who feel spiritually lost;
for those who feel trapped by emotional,
financial or political circumstances;
that in Christ they may find peace,
freedom and vitality.

Pause

Father of love: **remake our lives.**

Welcome into your kingdom, Father,
all who have died in faith,
and give them the joy of eternal life with you.

Pause

Father of love: **remake our lives.**

With deepest thankfulness
for all that makes our lives
so richly blest, we give you lasting praise.

**Accept these prayers
for the sake of your Son,
our Saviour Jesus Christ, Amen.**

3rd Sunday in Advent

Be prepared for the coming of the Lord. John the Baptist was the promised forerunner to Christ, and his teaching inspired many to turn back to God's ways, making them receptive when Jesus began his ministry. We, too, need to renounce sin and prepare for the time when Christ will come again in glory.

Let us bring to God our loving Father
all the cares that weigh on our hearts,
knowing that he understands us
better than we understand ourselves.

Father, we bring the daily work of those who labour to spread the good news of Christ amid apathy, ridicule or prejudice; may they be encouraged and strengthened.

Pause

Father, hear us: **and prepare us to meet you.**

Father, we bring our daily work, with all the pressures, monotony, enjoyment and mistakes;
help your world to recognise your presence
and trust in your love.

Pause

Father, hear us: **and prepare us to meet you.**

Father, we bring all our loved ones
with their hopes and disappointments,
their struggles and their successes;
may they be guided and nurtured by your love.

Pause

Father, hear us: **and prepare us to meet you.**

Father, we bring all those
whose lives seem to them bleak,
painful or empty of meaning;
please release them, unburden them,
and fill them with your gift of joy.

Pause

Father, hear us: **and prepare us to meet you.**

Father, we commend to your unfailing love
all who have died,
especially...

Pause

Father, hear us: **and prepare us to meet you.**

Filled with thankfulness for all
your many blessings to us,
we offer you our praise.
May we never forget your generosity.

Merciful Father
accept these prayers
for the sake of your Son,
our Saviour Jesus Christ, Amen.

4th Sunday in Advent

Mary was chosen by God to be the mother of Jesus, our Saviour. God's great sign of love is that he is carried through a human pregnancy and born into a human family which is descended from David. In this way the prophecies are fulfilled and God's glory revealed to the whole world.

Fellow travellers of Christ's Way,
as we walk together through life,
let us pray together in his Spirit.

Father, we bring to your love
all who serve Christ in his church;
that they may not flinch
from responding to their calling,
but rather abandon themselves
to your guidance and protection.

Pause

Heavenly Father: **let your will be done.**

Guide all who are in authority
throughout the world;
that they may be strengthened

to stand firm in what is right even if it is unpopular.

Pause

Heavenly Father: **let your will be done.**

Father, in your love we remember our own mothers,
all parents and foster parents,
all women in labour at this moment
and all who are pregnant;
that they may be blessed and supported.

Pause

Heavenly Father: **let your will be done.**

Father we commend to your love
those who have been rejected or abandoned
by their families or by society;
those who are constantly
ridiculed, criticised or badly treated;
may your love break down prejudice,
disperse hatred and build bridges of reconciliation.

Pause

Heavenly Father: **let your will be done.**

Father, into your hands we commend
all who have died and those who mourn.

Pause

Heavenly Father: **let your will be done.**

Father, our lives are so rich with all your blessings,
and we thank you for all your love.

**Accept these prayers for the sake of your Son,
our Saviour Jesus Christ, Amen.**

Christmas Day

Christ, our Saviour, is born. Eternal God breaks into human existence to transform and redeem it. In the darkness of night, God's majestic glory becomes a vulnerable newborn baby. Creator of all is entirely dependent on those he has created. Such is the measure of his infinite love.

As we gather to worship the Christchild,
born today,
let us pray trustfully
to our heavenly Father.

Father, we pray for all Christians
celebrating with us all over the world,
in all climates, times and seasons
as our planet turns.

Pause

Light of ages: **be born in our hearts.**

Father, we pray for all areas of darkness
where your light is desperately needed to bring peace,
understanding, sensitivity and compassion.

Pause

Light of ages: **be born in our hearts.**

Father, we commend to you our homes,
families, neighbours and friends;
all children and young babies, all being born today.

Pause

Light of ages: **be born in our hearts.**

We pray for those who are hungry, cold or homeless;
for all who are separated from their loved ones;
all who find the festivities of Christmas
emphasising their isolation and misery.

Pause

Light of ages: **be born in our hearts.**

We thank you for all who have
worshipped you throughout the ages;
for the lives and examples of all
who shone with your light
and now rest in your peace.

Pause

Light of ages: **be born in our hearts.**

Father in thankfulness we praise you;
accept these prayers
for the sake of your Son,
our Saviour Jesus Christ, Amen.

1st Sunday after Christmas

We can see the great love of God personally in Jesus, the Christ. All the promises and hopes are fulfilled by the birth of this baby in Bethlehem, because he is the one who can set us free from our slavery to all that is evil. His salvation, beginning in Israel, extends outwards to include every created person.

Let us pray to God our Father
because he loves us so dearly.

We pray that the light of the world
may shine so brightly in our lives
that other people notice it
and are attracted to you
by the way we live and love.

Pause

Father, live among us: **live through our lives.**

We pray that our world may stop
its noise, chatter and arguing
long enough to hear the angels
singing of hope and peace.

Pause

Father, live among us: **live through our lives.**

Father, we pray for our families
and all our friends and neighbours;
may every relationship we have
be filled with your love.

<u>Pause</u>

Father, live among us: **live through our lives.**

We pray for the homeless and all refugees and exiles;
for children from broken homes,
and all who are destitute, malnourished or ill.

<u>Pause</u>

Father, live among us: **live through our lives.**

We pray for all from whom we are separated now
through death;
may they live in your light for ever
and may their loved ones know your comfort.

<u>Pause</u>

Father, live among us: **live through our lives.**

Father, we can never thank you enough
for coming to rescue us,
and we praise you now and in our lives;
merciful Father
accept these prayers
for the sake of your Son,
our Saviour Jesus Christ, Amen.

2nd Sunday after Christmas

God's Son, Jesus, shared with us all the experience of childhood. He grew up in a family which had its share of troubles as well as joys, and his love can fill our family life if we invite him to live among us in our homes.

My brothers and sisters in Christ,
as members of one family let us talk to God our Father
about our needs, cares and concerns.

We pray for the life, teaching and fellowship
of the Church, our Christian family;
help us to support and care for one another
as true family members,
regardless of physical, cultural
or intellectual differences.

Pause

God our Father: **hear your children's prayer.**

We pray for friendship and good will
between all the different nations in our world;

teach us to enjoy the variety as richness,
rather than fearing it as a threat.

Pause

God our Father: **hear your children's prayer.**

We ask for your blessing and guidance
in all the homes of this parish;
as each problem and difficulty arises
may your loving wisdom steer us in the right direction.

Pause

God our Father: **hear your children's prayer.**

We pray for all who have been damaged
by a disturbed or violent upbringing;
for children who are growing up
amid hatred and cruelty;
may they be healed by love.

Pause

God our Father: **hear your children's prayer.**

We pray for those who have recently died
and commend them into your
everlasting care and protection.

Pause

God our Father: **hear your children's prayer.**

We thank you for all the joys and blessings in our lives;
especially we thank you for the relationships
which enrich our lives so much.
We ask you to make your home
in our hearts and homes,
and accept these prayers for the sake of your Son,
our Saviour Jesus Christ, Amen.

The Epiphany of our Lord

Wise men from distant countries were led to worship Jesus. The light of the living Christ also leads us, and when our lives reflect his light, many others will be drawn to worship the true God who made us and loves us.

Fellow travellers of Christ's Way,
let us pray together for the church and for the world.

Father, may our Christian witness,
in a confused and nervous world,
shine with a piercing integrity and warmth
that awakens people's hearts to the love of their creator.

Pause

Light of the nations: **shine in our lives.**

Bless and protect all travellers and pilgrims;
teach us to cherish the beauty of our world
and share its riches.

Pause

Light of the nations: **shine in our lives.**

Help us to see Christ in the eyes of all those we meet,
and delight in giving you glory
by serving others without expecting rewards.

Pause

Light of the nations: **shine in our lives.**

Direct our vision to see
the best practical ways of providing shelter
for the homeless, safe accommodation
for those who live in fear of violence,
and food for the hungry.

Pause

Light of the nations: **shine in our hearts.**

May all who have died in faith
be bathed in the everlasting light
of your loving presence,
and may those who mourn be comforted.

Pause

Light of the nations: **shine in our hearts.**

In thankfulness, Father,
we offer you our lives.
**Accept these prayers
for the sake of your Son,
our Saviour Jesus Christ, Amen.**

1st Sunday after the Epiphany

Jesus is anointed at his baptism with the Holy Spirit. When we are baptised we are born again into new and lasting life. We are then given the power and all necessary ingredients for witnessing to God's love wherever he sends us. Together we work towards his kingdom which is founded on caring love.

My companions in Christ, let us quieten our hearts before God our Father, and pray together for the needs of the church and the world.

We bring to you, Lord, all who preach
and teach the Christian message of salvation,
and those who hear it; through your Spirit,
may its reality, truth and hope take root and grow.

Pause

Father of Jesus: **use us for your glory.**

We bring to you, Lord, our stewardship
of the world's resources; all discussions and councils
where far-reaching decisions are made
concerning government, conservation,
international relations, methods of harnessing power,

and fighting diseases; may your generous will prevail
over human greed and prejudice.

Pause

Father of Jesus: **use us for your glory.**

We bring to you, Lord, all who are apathetic,
mentally exhausted or aimlessly wandering through life;
all who are eaten up with jealousy,
poisoned by hate or weighed down by guilt;
may they feel and know the warmth and depth
of your love, and your yearning for their peace.

Pause

Father of Jesus: **use us for your glory.**

We bring to you, Lord, ourselves,
our friends and all we shall meet during this week,
however briefly; fill us with your love so that others
may see it and be drawn towards their Saviour.

Pause

Father of Jesus: **use us for your glory.**

We bring to you, Lord, the dying and those
who have already passed into the next stage of life;
may they live forever in your peace.

Pause

Father of Jesus: **use us for your glory.**

Father, we rejoice in your uncompromising love for us,
and thank you for all the blessings
we receive from you each day.
**Accept these prayers for the sake of your Son,
Our Saviour Jesus Christ, Amen**

2nd Sunday after the Epiphany

The calling of the first disciples. Just as God called the prophets through the ages and the apostles by name to work with him for the good of the world, so we are chosen and called to work in partnership with God for the growth of his kingdom.

Bound together in the life of Christ
let us pour out our needs and concerns
before our Lord and Father,
who knows and loves us so well.
Father, we commend to your love
all ministers of your Word and sacrament;
keep them true to their calling
so that their life and work
brings many into contact with you.

Pause

Lord, here I am: **I come to do your will.**

Father, we commend to your wisdom
all who wield power;
help them to encourage reconciliation
rather than revenge, friendship rather than aggression,

and flexibility rather than stubborn intransigence.

Pause

Lord, here I am: **I come to do your will.**

Father, we commend to your peace and joy
our homes and all the homes in this parish,
especially any where there is conflict or distress;
dwell with us, so that our homes speak
to every visitor of your love.

Pause

Lord, here I am: **I come to do your will.**

Father, we commend to your healing
all who are in pain or danger;
all who are recovering from surgery;
all who depend on others for life and movement;
and who long for a friend who would visit them
and care about them.

Pause

Lord, here I am: **I come to do your will.**

Father, we commend to your keeping
those who have left this life through the gate of death;
may they live with you in the light of heaven for ever.

Pause

Loving Father, we thank you for calling us
and we offer you the rest of our lives.
**Accept these prayers
for the sake of your Son,
our Saviour Jesus Christ, Amen.**

35

3rd Sunday after the Epiphany

Through signs and miracles God's glory is shown. Throughout the Old Testament God proves his love for his people by the care and protection he lavishes on them, and as Jesus heals, feeds and encourages his way through the Gospel, we become aware of his glory—the glory of God himself.

Companions in Christ, as we remember with gratitude
all that God has done for us,
let us bring to his love the needs and concerns
of the Church and of the world.

We bring to your love, Lord,
the daily work of each member of Christ's body;
that in constant prayer we may learn your will
and your way of doing things,
until we work exclusively for your glory.

Pause

In you we trust: **we look to you for help.**

We bring to your love, Lord, the mistakes,
short-sightedness and arrogance of our world;
that in Christ we may learn to respect one another

and the treasures of the planet we inhabit.

Pause

In you we trust: **we look to you for help.**

We bring to your love, Lord, the wounded
and the afraid, the despairing and the rejected;
that they may find Christ suffering alongside them
and allow him to restore them to wholeness.

Pause

In you we trust: **we look to you for help.**

We bring to your love, Lord,
our busy concern with unimportant things;
that in spending more time in Christ's company
we may learn to act and react in all our relationships
with the character and Spirit of Jesus.

Pause

In you we trust: **we look to you for help.**

We bring to your love, Lord, all our dear ones
who are separated from us through death;
that as children of eternity we may always remember
how close they are, linked by your eternal love.

Pause

In you we trust: **we look to you for help.**

Almighty Father, hear the prayers we offer,
and use our bodies, minds and spirits
in establishing your kingdom.
**Accept these prayers for the sake of your Son,
our Saviour Jesus Christ, Amen.**

4th Sunday after the Epiphany

God shows his glory in our lives by renewing us from the inside and transforming us completely. As we increase our availability to the life-giving power of God, we shall become more and more like him, and reflect his glory more and more brightly.

As members of the body of Christ
bound together in his love, let us pray together now,
confident in God's promise to be amongst us.

We pray for all who form the church
in its variety and richness throughout the world;
may the weak be encouraged and strengthened,
the wanderers return, those besieged by doubt
be given the assurance of faith,
and the jaded refreshed by your living Spirit.

Pause

Take us as we are: **and use us, Lord.**

We pray for all councils, committees
and governing bodies, for those serving on juries,
for air, sea and mountain rescue teams;
that in working together in your strength

they may strive for what is good, just and honest,
so that your will is accomplished in them.

Pause

Take us as we are: **and use us, Lord.**

We pray for our families and our friends,
that we may be transformed and renewed
through the richness of your presence;
give us deeper insight, more awareness
and greater love for one another.

Pause

Take us as we are: **and use us, Lord.**

We pray for the poor and for the hungry,
for all frustrated by damaged or crippled bodies;
for those in prison, and those enslaved
by drugs, alcohol, hatred or fear.

Pause

Take us as we are: **and use us, Lord.**

We pray for those who have died and those who are at
present on that last journey; may they have peace
in the joy of your presence for ever.

Pause

Take us as we are: **and use us, Lord.**
Father, we thank you for all your glory in the world
you have made, for all you have accomplished
in our lives and in the lives of the saints;
we lay the rest of our lives at your feet.
**Accept these prayers for the sake of your Son,
Our Saviour Jesus Christ, Amen.**

5th Sunday after the Epiphany

The wisdom of God is revealed to us clearly in Jesus. Through all the problems and decision making of our lives we have God's assurance that he will lead us to make good choices and act wisely and well, provided we remain rooted in the loving wisdom of our Lord.

Fellow travellers of the Way of Christ,
we know that God our Father loves us;
let us therefore pray to him now about
all that concerns us in his church and in the world.

We pray for the many groups of Christians
worshipping alongside us,
but in other communities and in other countries;
for all who risk persecution for their faith;
that we may support and encourage one another
and serve the world as Christ's body,
whatever the personal cost.

Pause

Take us, Father: **and live through our lives.**

We pray for the leaders of the nations, all members
of governments and their financial and social advisers;

that they may be led in the Spirit of Wisdom
to work in harmony with God's will
so his values are reflected in all policy making.

Pause

Take us, Father: **and live through our lives.**

We pray for a lessening of selfishness
and a broadening of our characters,
until we are prepared to welcome,
love and care for whoever is in need,
working hand in hand with God wherever we are sent.

Pause

Take us, Father: **and live through our lives.**

We pray for all in intensive care at the moment;
all undergoing emergency surgery;
all women in labour and their babies;
all who are approaching death;
that God's great healing love may wash through
their bodies and minds in a surge of peace.

Pause

Take us, Father: **and live through our lives.**

Father, we thank you for your constant,
loving provision for us throughout our lives,
and commend to your safe keeping for ever
all who have died, especially...

Merciful Father,
**accept these prayers for the sake of your Son,
our Saviour Jesus Christ, Amen.**

6th Sunday after the Epiphany

God's character is revealed through parables to all who seek to know him more clearly. Jesus often used the form of parables—stories with hidden meanings—as an aid to teaching people about God and the Kingdom of Heaven.

Rooted in Christ, let us call to mind now
all those in need, and pray for them
to our heavenly Father.

Lord, we pray that all who teach the Christian faith
may be given appropriate language
to get through to those who hear them,
so that the Word of God takes root in many hearts.

Pause

Lord of life: **teach us your ways.**

May all diplomats and negotiators promote
peace and friendship between the nations,
fostering mutual respect and understanding.

Pause

Lord of life: **teach us your ways.**

May we and our families, neighbours and friends
become daily more Christlike and less self-centred;
more responsive to the needs of those around us
and less bothered by what we get out of life.

Pause

Lord of life: **teach us your ways.**

May those whose lives have been threatened
or shattered by crippling illness or injury
find new doors opening, new hope appearing
and new meaning transforming their outlook.

Pause

Lord of life: **teach us your ways.**

May those who have passed from this life
into eternity rejoice for ever
in the fullness of your glory.

Lord, we thank you for dealing with us so patiently
and with such compassion;
if we should close our hearts to your will
please keep knocking until we open the door!

Merciful Father
**accept these prayers
for the sake of your Son,
our Saviour Jesus Christ, Amen.**

9th Sunday before Easter

Christ the teacher. Not only with his words, but in his life Jesus shows us how to live fulfilled and fruitful lives, realising our potential and playing our part in bringing the world to wholeness.

Chosen by God to be members of his body,
let us gather our cares and concerns
and bring them before our heavenly Father
who loves us and knows us personally.

We pray for the many individuals
comprising the body of Christ,
with all their varied ministries;
for those unsure of God's plan for them;
may your will be made clear to them
and may they be given courage to accept your call.

Pause

Lord, nourish us: **that we may bear fruit.**

We pray for the world and its areas of conflict,
political unrest, decadence and deceit;
that Christ, the Lord of all truth and life,

may lead humanity to desire justice, peace and integrity.

Pause
Lord, nourish us: **that we may bear fruit.**

We pray for a deeper trust in God among all of us here,
and the families we represent; that we may spend
our lives in getting to know you better,
so we reflect your light more brightly
and can be of greater use to you in serving your world.

Pause
Lord, nourish us: **that we may bear fruit.**

We pray for the bereaved and all who mourn;
for those who have miscarried or given birth
to a stillborn baby; for those who feel uncared for
and unloved; for those who must watch their children
die from lack of food.

Pause
Lord, nourish us: **that we may bear fruit.**

We pray for all the faithful who have died;
may they rest for ever in the peace and joy of heaven.

We offer you our thanks and praise for the way you
have guided us and brought us to worship you now;
may we continue to praise you
in the way we live the rest of our lives.

Merciful Father
**accept these prayers for the sake of your Son,
our Saviour Jesus Christ, Amen.**

8th Sunday before Easter

Jesus the healer. The prophets had foretold the time when God's healing love would renew and restore, and whenever holy men and women became channels of God's power, acts of healing had occurred which directed the people's praise towards the God of creation and renewal. Now, in Jesus, God walks among his people, restoring them to wholeness.

My brothers and sisters in Christ,
knowing the deep love that surrounds us
and reaches out to us in every distress,
let us unload our burdens of care
to the healing power of our heavenly Father.

We bring before you the Church's work
among the homeless, the disillusioned
and the apathetic,
in parish communities all over the world.

Pause

Life-giving Lord: **hear us and help us, we pray.**

We bring before you all areas of the world
where lack of communication

breeds suspicion and fear; where lack of understanding
breeds insecurity and a spirit of revenge.

Pause

Life-giving Lord: **hear us and help us, we pray.**

We bring before you each member of this community,
each individual anxiety and sorrow,
each hope and dream,
each weakness and special need.

Pause

Life-giving Lord: **hear us and help us, we pray.**

We bring before you all whose lives
are crippled by unrepented sin or the refusal to forgive;
all whose lives are constantly restless
and devoid of peace.

Pause

Life-giving Lord: **hear us and help us, we pray.**

We bring before you those who have died
and those who miss them.

Pause

Life-giving Lord: **hear us and help us, we pray.**

We bring before you the joy and happiness
of our daily life,
the blessings that lift our hearts to praise you.

Merciful Father
**accept these prayers for the sake of your Son,
our Saviour Jesus Christ, Amen.**

7th Sunday before Easter

Jesus Christ is the friend of sinners. The bad news about being human is that we seem to find it so easy to hurt one another and indulge in our selfishness; with even the best of intentions, we fail and sin. The good news is that in Jesus, God meets us where we are, loves us, warts and all, and brings about reconciliation, forgiveness and peace.

Fellow members of Christ,
let us approach our heavenly Father,
acknowledging the wonder of his involvement with us,
and asking him to help us.

We pray for all who labour to spread the Good News
especially those who face threatening behaviour,
imprisonment or persecution;
for those who are tempted to remain silent
in order to avoid danger to themselves or their families;
that they may be given your courage and your peace.

Pause

Lord, in our weakness: **we ask for your help.**

We pray for all the injustice, cruelty
and oppression of our world; its confusion of priorities,
its lost opportunities and misdirected zeal;

that we may be guided unceasingly by the level-headed,
compassionate leadership of God's Spirit.

Pause

Lord, in our weakness: **we ask for your help.**

We pray for our families, friends and neighbours;
for the very young and the very old in our care;
for wisdom to see opportunities of Christ's love,
and for enough energy and time
to do what God needs us to.

Pause

Lord, in our weakness: **we ask for your help.**

We pray for all who are wounded and injured—
those in hospital and all in pain; that they may find
Christ among them in their suffering;
we pray for those who inflict pain on others;
for terrorists, murderers and all
who are fired with hatred; that their lives may be
transformed by encountering Christ.

Pause

Lord, in our weakness: **we ask for your help.**

We pray for those on the verge of death
and those who have passed into eternity;
may they rest in your peace for ever.

We give you thanks for all your care and healing love.
Merciful Father
**accept these prayers for the sake of your Son,
our Saviour Jesus Christ, Amen.**

Almighty and everlasting God, you hate nothing that
you have made, and forgive the sins of all those who are
penitent. Create and make in us new and contrite
hearts that lamenting our sins and acknowledging
our wretchedness we may receive from you, the God of
all mercy, perfect forgiveness and peace, through

Jesus
Christ
our
Lord.

Ash Wednesday

Reconciliation with God. This will involve first
admitting our need of God's mercy and
forgiveness and then examining our lives in his
light to see what needs to be done. God does not
simply patch up the bits of us that look bad—
he completely renews and restores, giving us the
joy and peace of forgiveness.

Let us come before God, our creator and sustainer,
with the needs of the church and of the world.

We bring to your love, O Lord,
all who have committed their lives to your service;
that they may all be one,
bound together by your Holy Spirit.

Pause

Father of mercy: **hear us with compassion.**

We bring to your love all the areas of the world
in which there is hostility and unrest;
that new routes to negotiation
and reconciliation may emerge.

Pause

Father of mercy: **hear us with compassion.**

We bring to your love
the members of our human families,
especially any we find difficult
to get on with or understand;
that our love for one another
may enter a new dimension
of warm and positive caring, seasoned with laughter.

Pause

Father of mercy: **hear us with compassion.**

We bring to your love
all who have become hard and aggressive
through years of festering hate or jealousy;
that their unresolved conflicts
may be brought to your light and healed.

Pause

Lord of mercy: **hear us with compassion.**

We bring to your love all those, dear to us,
who are separated from us by death;
may we come, one day, with them
to share the eternal peace and joy of heaven.

Pause

Lord of mercy: **hear us with compassion.**

We thank you for all your blessings and patient loving,
and especially for coming to save us from our sin.

Merciful Father
**accept these prayers for the sake of your Son,
our Saviour Jesus Christ, Amen.**

1st Sunday in Lent

Temptation. Man and woman spoilt God's perfect creation by falling into temptation and disobeying their creator. We are all guilty of sin, but through Christ we are given the strength and grace to resist temptation just as he did.

Trusting not in our weakness but in God's mercy
let us pray to him now.

We pray for Christians whose faith
is being tested by hardship,
spiritual dryness or any outside pressures;
that they may hold fast to you, Lord Christ,
and emerge stronger in the knowledge
of your loyal, sustaining love.

Pause

Lord, you are the rock: **on whom our security rests.**

We pray for those involved in advertising;
broadcasting and journalism,
and for all in the entertainment business;

that they may not encourage selfishness or violence,
but discretion and insight.

Pause

Lord, you are the rock: **on whom our security rests.**

We pray for the people on either side of us now;
for the families represented here,
and all who live in the same street as we do;
that we may live out the pattern
of Christlike loving in a practical way.

Pause

Lord, you are the rock: **on whom our security rests.**

We pray for those blinded by prejudice
or self-centred thinking; for those being dragged down
by a drug or alcohol habit they feel powerless to stop;
that they may be led tenderly to freedom.

Pause

Lord, you are the rock: **on whom our security rests.**

We pray for those who,
having worshipped you on earth,
have now past into eternity;
may they spend eternity in unending love and praise.

Pause

Lord, you are the rock: **on whom our security rests.**

Father, we thank you
for showing us the way to abundant life.
Merciful Father,
accept these prayers for the sake of your Son,
our Saviour Jesus Christ, Amen.

2nd Sunday in Lent

Conflict between right and wrong. We need discernment to recognise God's will on our journey through an often confusing and disturbing world. Following Jesus demands both trust and calm, and level-headed assessment of anyone setting him or herself up as a prophet or spiritual leader. If we learn to look with the eyes of Christ, we shall not be led astray.

Followers of the Way of Christ,
let us bring to the Lord the needs of our times.

Father, we pray for your blessing
on all who confess belief in you;
that they may witness powerfully
to your unselfish love and humility
by the way they act and the lives they lead.

Pause
Father, lead us: **free us from all that is evil.**

Father, we pray for your blessing
on all who administer justice;
those working in Law Courts and serving on juries,
and those who make laws;

that they may be given insight and integrity.

Pause

Father, lead us: **free us from all that is evil.**

Father, we pray for your blessing on us during this Lent
as we examine our lives and draw closer to you;
that through our self-discipline and prayer
we may enter your stillness and know your will for us.

Pause

Father, lead us: **free us from all that is evil.**

Father, we pray for your blessing on all in prison
or on probation; on those living in acute poverty
or in refugee camps; on all who work among them
to heal, redirect, support and encourage.

Pause

Father, lead us: **free us from all that is evil.**

Father, we pray for your blessing
on those who have passed through death, especially...
may we one day share with them
eternal life in your presence.

Pause

Father, lead us: **free us from all that is evil.**

In silence, Father, we bring to you
our individual concerns and joys.

Pause

Merciful Father
**accept these prayers for the sake of your Son,
our Saviour Jesus Christ, Amen.**

3rd Sunday in Lent

Good news about suffering. In Christ, suffering can become a positive experience; a route to full life and deeper understanding. In fact, Jesus goes so far as to say it is a necessary part of our life in him. He will be there with us all through the very blackest, bleakest times.

As children and heirs through adoption, and knowing that Jesus shares in all our suffering and joy, let us confide in our heavenly Father who knows us so well.

Father, into your enlightenment and perception we bring all whose faith is limited by fear or prejudice; all whose living faith has been replaced by the empty shell of habit.

Pause

Father, give us courage: **you are our only strength.**

Father, into the depths of your wisdom and understanding we bring those with responsibilities, and all who have difficult decisions to make; all those in charge of hospitals, schools, industry and all community services.

Pause

Father, give us courage: **you are our only strength.**

Into your tireless faithfulness we bring any
who rely on us for help, support or guidance;
any whom we are being asked to serve
or introduce to your love.

Pause

Father, give us courage: **you are our only strength.**

Into the gentleness of your healing love we bring all
who are in pain; all those recovering from surgery;
those involved in crippling accidents
or suffering from wasting diseases.

Pause

Father, give us courage: **you are our only strength.**

Into your light and peace we commend
those who have died, especially any dear to us
whom we name in the silence of our hearts.

Pause

Father, give us courage: **you are our only strength.**

Father, we thank you for supporting us
and encouraging us when life is hard,
and for all the exuberant vitality
of the world you have created for us to live in.

Merciful Father
**accept these prayers for the sake of your Son,
our Saviour Jesus Christ, Amen.**

4th Sunday in Lent

God's glory is shown in Jesus at the transfiguration. The disciples were given a glimpse of Jesus' divinity which strengthened their faith and upheld them. Through their account, we also become witnesses: Jesus is indeed the Son of God.

In faith, knowing that where two or three are gathered
in your name you have promised to be among them,
let our minds and hearts be filled
with stillness as we pray.

We pray for the Church;
that all your ministers may be given
perception and understanding,
to lead people into the light of your truth.

Pause

Lord of glory: **make us more like you.**

We pray for all councils, committees and conferences;
that a spirit of integrity may underlie all discussion and
a desire for goodness inspire all decisions.

Pause

Lord of glory: **make us more like you.**

We pray for all families,
especially those who have troubles;
that they may not be damaged through their suffering,
but rather grow in compassion and understanding.

Pause
Lord of glory: **make us more like you.**

We pray for those in pain and distress;
for the mentally, physically and emotionally disabled;
that they may be comforted and strengthened
by your presence, trusting in your love
which never fails.

Pause
Lord of glory: **make us more like you.**

We pray for the dying and those who have
already moved on from this world into eternity;
may they rest for ever in your peace.

Pause
Lord of glory: **make us more like you.**

In thankfulness and praise we remember
all your many blessings, given to us each day,
and ask you to help us become
more generous-hearted and appreciative.

Pause
Lord of glory: **make us more like you.**

Merciful Father
**accept these prayers for the sake of your Son,
our Saviour Jesus Christ, Amen.**

5th Sunday in Lent

The victory of the cross. Nothing could look more like failure than the crucifixion, as the promising healer and teacher hung suffering at the mercy of mankind. Yet it was through this anguish and pain, offered in love without sin, that our salvation was secured for ever.

In the presence of God, the giver of all life,
let us lift our hearts and pray.

We pray for all who are training
for ministry in your church;
may they grow in wisdom and humility,
and be increasingly filled with the life
you have won for us.

Pause

Lord, breathe into us: **that we may live.**

We pray for all areas of bureaucracy
which frustrate and delay the course of useful action;
for areas where anarchy undermines stability;
for areas of political corruption;
that whatever is good may flourish and grow,

so evil is rendered powerless and overthrown.

Pause
Lord, breathe into us: **that we may live.**

We pray for all who are engaged or newly married;
for those coping with family problems,
difficult circumstances or bereavement;
may they lean on your loving presence
which dispels all fear, and brings life and peace.

Pause
Lord, breathe into us: **that we may live.**

We pray that your calming reassurance
will bring peace of mind and spirit
to those worried about the future,
those dreading some difficult event,
and those who are frightened of dying.

Pause
Lord, breathe into us: **that we may live.**

We thank you for the life and example
of all who have lived, worked and died
in the joy of your service; may we one day
share with them eternal life in your presence.

Pause
Lord, breathe into us: **that we may live.**

Father, with thankful hearts we offer these concerns
for the church and for the world.
**Accept these prayers for the sake of your Son,
our Saviour Jesus Christ, Amen.**

Palm Sunday

Jesus enters Jerusalem as the Prince of Peace,
riding on a donkey. At the heart of our rejoicing
is the pain he is bound to suffer in redeeming us
through unflinching love. Yet we still certainly
rejoice, for we know he has won the victory.
Jesus is indeed our King.

Fellow pilgrims, as we welcome Jesus
and hail him as our King, let us offer to God our Father
in prayer the deep concerns and needs
of the Church and of the world.

We bring to your love all who are baptised,
and especially those who have lost their faith
or have stopped praying; may they be brought back
through your love, and put into contact with those
who can guide and reassure them.

Pause

Lord, uphold us: **give us your strength.**

We bring to your love every meeting, demonstration,
convention and all large crowds; may they be peaceful
and ordered, inspiring those present for good,

rather than inciting them to violence.

Pause

Lord, uphold us: **give us your strength.**

We bring to your love our own loved ones,
the members of our families, our friends
and especially those from whom we are separated,
either by distance or death;
and all who are missing from their homes;
may your powerful love protect us from all that is evil.

Pause

Lord, uphold us: **give us your strength.**

We bring to your love those suffering
from incurable or life-threatening diseases;
those who need medical care, but are either too poor,
or live too far away to receive it;
make us more ready to help
with our time, money and influence,
so that unnecessary suffering and death are avoided.

Pause

Lord, uphold us: **give us your strength.**

We bring to your love those who have died;
may they rest in the light and joy
of your presence for ever.

Father, may we praise you not only with our voices
but also in the lives we lead.
Merciful Father
**accept these prayersfor the sake of your Son,
our Saviour Jesus Christ, Amen.**

Maundy Thursday

The new Covenant between God and his people. The Passover feast was an annual celebration of God freeing his people from slavery. The blood of the lamb protected them, and was both a sacrifice and food before their journey. Now Christ offers himself in the bread and wine and in the washing of feet. His sacrifice frees us from sin's slavery.

We belong to the body of Christ.
In his name let us pray to the Father
for the Church and for the world.

We commend to your care and protection
all who are abused, imprisoned or insulted
because of their faith.

Pause

Lord, by your example: **teach us all to love.**

We commend to your light and truth
all governments and committees,
every head of state, and all leaders.

Pause

Lord, by your example: **teach us all to love.**

We commend to your longsuffering patience
and compassion, ourselves,
with our frequent misuse of his blessings
and failure to serve.

Pause
Lord, by your example: **teach us all to love.**

We commend to your healing and wholeness
all who are ill or injured;
those undergoing surgery
and those nearing death.

Pause
Lord, by your example: **teach us all to love.**

We commend to your light and lasting peace
all those who have died, especially...

We thank you, Lord,
for all your guidance and loving care;
fulfil our needs in the way which is best for us
in the context of eternity.

Merciful Father
**accept these prayers
for the sake of your Son,
our Saviour Jesus Christ, Amen.**

Good Friday

Jesus lays down his life for us. He yearns so much for us to be saved that he undergoes death, allowing the burden of the whole world's evil to rest on his shoulders. Not once does he stop loving or forgiving. His death is no failure, but a victory of cosmic proportions, through which we are saved.

As children of our heavenly Father,
and knowing the extent of his love for us,
let us pray to him now.

We pray for all whom you have called to serve you,
in different ministries and in every country;
may they work in your strength
and show your love and compassion.

Pause

Lord, how you must love us:
may we love you more and more

We pray for all in positions of authority,
particularly when faced with moral dilemmas
and the temptation to act expediently;
may they see what is right

and be encouraged to stand firm.

Pause

Lord, how you must love us:
may we love you more and more.

We pray for the members of our family
and all whom we love and care for;
may we always be ready to forgive,
respect and value them.

Pause

Lord, how you must love us:
may we love you more and more.

We pray for all who know the pain
of rejection, vulnerability or torture;
for all innocent sufferers
and prisoners of conscience;
may they know your love for them.

Pause

Lord, how you must love us:
may we love you more and more.

We pray for those who are nearing death
and those who have moved on into eternity;
may we one day be welcomed into your kingdom.

Lord, how can we ever thank you
for what you have done for us!
May our lives proclaim our thanks and praise.

Merciful Father
**accept these prayers for the sake of your Son,
Our Saviour Jesus Christ, Amen.**

Easter Day

Jesus is risen from the dead! Having passed through death to life, Christ has won the victory over everything evil and destructive. Full of glory and power, he enables us to bring the hope and joy of resurrection into the world's problems and tragedies. With God, nothing is impossible.

In the joy of this Easter morning let us pray to the God who loves us completely.

We pray that the joy and conviction of Christians
may be so radiant
that all who are lost, weary and searching
may be directed towards your lasting, inner peace.

Pause

Risen Lord: **live in us all.**

We pray that from every world crisis
and tragedy some good may come;
every problem become an opportunity
for development and spiritual growth.

Pause

Risen Lord: **live in us all.**

We pray for the newly born,
and for all families,
that the children may be nurtured,
and the elderly cherished
through your wide, accepting love.

Pause
Risen Lord: **live in us all.**

We pray that those in mental,
physical or spiritual distress
may recognise in their suffering
a privilege of sharing Christ's passion,
until they also share
the joy of new life in you.

Pause
Risen Lord: **live in us all.**

We pray that all those who have died
may share your risen life for ever.

Pause
Risen **Lord: live in us all.**

In silence we praise you, Father,
for your abundant blessings.

Merciful Father
accept these prayers
for the sake of your Son,
our Saviour Jesus Christ, Amen.

1st Sunday after Easter

The life-giving presence of the risen Lord. The disciples began to realise that Jesus was present with them whether they could see him or not. We, too, experience his spiritual presence among us and welcome him with joy.

Dear friends in Christ, as we gather here in the presence of the living God, let us ask for his help and guidance in the Church and in the world.

We join in prayer with all other worshipping Christians; give us an increasing love and affection between individuals and groups in every parish and denomination; increasing open-heartedness, outreach and generosity of spirit.

Pause

Unchanging Lord: **we pledge ourselves to your service.**

We pray for the breaking down of suspicion, double standards and hypocrisy in our world; that the nations may work together to conquer the problems of food and water distribution, so that our planet's resources are shared and not wasted.

Pause
Unchanging Lord: **we pledge ourselves to your service.**

We pray for the homes and families represented here,
with all their particular joys and sorrows,
needs and resources;
that our lives may be practical witnesses to our faith.

Pause
Unchanging Lord: **we pledge ourselves to your service.**

We pray for those involved in medical research,
and all who suffer from diseases
which are as yet incurable;
for any who are too weak or exhausted to pray;
for any who are desperate or suicidal.

Pause
Unchanging Lord: **we pledge ourselves to your service.**

We pray that all who have died in faith
may rise to new life in glory.

Father, we thank you for your immense compassion,
understanding and encouragement throughout our lives.

Merciful Father
**accept these prayers for the sake of your Son,
our Saviour Jesus Christ, Amen.**

2nd Sunday after Easter

Jesus leads and teaches us his ways like a good shepherd. We recognise his voice and he knows each of us by name. Just as he led the disciples, on the road to Emmaus, to the point where they recognised him in the breaking of bread, so he leads us, his sheep, to know him and trust him.

Rejoicing in the amazing love of God our Father,
let us pour out to him our needs, cares and concerns.

Good Shepherd, as we see, with sorrow,
the divisions between Christian groups,
we ask you to enable us to become one flock.

Pause

Father, hear us: **and help us to hear you.**

As we see the glaring injustices of wealth
and food distribution in our world,
we ask you to give us courage to work in your strength
towards building a safer and more caring society.

Pause

Father, hear us: **and help us to hear you.**

As we watch our children growing up and our parents
growing older and feel anxious for their future,
we ask you for the assurance of your steadfast love,
and we entrust their lives to your perfect care.

Pause

Father, hear us: **and help us to hear you.**

As we see and read in the news
of all those afflicted by natural disasters,
by terrible accidents and by war,
we ask you, O Lord of life,
to bring good out of every evil
and growth out of every suffering.

Pause

Father, hear us: **and help us to hear you.**

As we remember our loved ones
who have passed through death into eternity,
we ask you to welcome them into your light and joy
for ever.

Pause

Father, hear us: **and help us to hear you.**

Loving Lord, we thank you
for the many joys and blessings you give us each day,
and for this opportunity to worship you.

Merciful Father
accept these prayers
for the sake of your Son,
our Saviour Jesus Christ, Amen.

3rd Sunday after Easter

Jesus is the resurrection and the life. Not only does he live for ever—he is actually life. When we put our trust in him, we become part of that full, complete life, which death will not destroy.

Filled with the hope and joy of the resurrection,
let us pray confidently to our loving Father.

We pray for the newly baptised and their families;
for those who are sensing God's call
and need reassurance in it;
for all God's people in every part of the world.

Pause

Life-giving Lord: **reign in our hearts.**

We pray for the areas in which there is fighting,
unrest and unresolved conflict;
for the unprincipled, the corrupt
and those who thirst for revenge.

Pause

Life-giving Lord: **reign in our hearts.**

We pray for our neighbours here; in our street;
and at school and at work; for those
with whom we live; for any who may be wishing
they knew someone willing to be friendly
and share their burden.

Pause

Life-giving Lord: **reign in our hearts.**

We pray for those finding life very trying
and difficult at the moment;
for those who are coping with personal tragedy,
heartache or mourning;
for all who are ill or frail.

Pause

Life-giving Lord: **reign in our hearts**

We pray for all who have died;
that they may rise to eternal life in the light of heaven.

Pause

Life-giving Lord: **reign in our hearts.**

Father, in so many ways we have been richly blessed;
give us thankful hearts and make us more appreciative
of all that is good in life.

Merciful Father
accept these prayers
for the sake of your Son,
our Saviour Jesus Christ, Amen.

4th Sunday after Easter

Jesus is the Way, the Truth and the Life. As we follow in his footsteps we experience the fellowship of his company, which gives us both courage to do his work and also peace of mind, even when life is difficult.

My companions in Christ, as we gather
in the great hope of our risen Lord who leads us,
let us pray to God who has shown us such patient love.

We pray for unity among all who follow
the Way of Christ; that in keeping our eyes
fixed on him we may be enabled to dissolve barriers,
to forgive and be reconciled, through the healing
power of accepting love.

Pause

Lord, guide us: **to do things your way.**

We pray for all in positions of responsibility and
leadership,
both internationally and in our own community; that
they may themselves be led by your Spirit to make wise

decisions and help create a humane and caring world.

Pause

Lord, guide us: **to do things your way.**

We pray for our homes and families,
with their hopes and sorrows,
difficulties and celebrations; that all our relationships
may be bathed in your love and compassion.

Pause

Lord, guide us: **to do things your way.**

We pray for those who incite others
to antisocial or criminal behaviour;
for all involved in drugs traffic; that they may open
their hearts and allow you to transform and heal;
for the weak, lonely, young and depressed
who are so vulnerable to their temptations;
give them help and strength to resist
the pressures on and around them.

Pause

Lord, guide us: **to do things your way.**

We pray that those who have died in faith
may be welcomed into the eternal joy of heaven,
to live with you for ever.

We thank you for all the richness of this beautiful
world, for the gift of life and time to spend;
for the example and companionship of Jesus.

Merciful Father
**accept these prayers for the sake of your Son,
our Saviour Jesus Christ, Amen.**

5th Sunday after Easter

Nothing can ever separate us from God's love.
Our new life in the risen Christ is a journey
home to the Father, and since God is on our side
we need not be anxious and afraid, no matter
what may happen to us on the way.

My Christian sisters and brothers, as we rejoice
at being called and chosen by our heavenly Father,
let us speak with him of our needs and concerns.

Father, we commend to your love
all leaders and teachers in the Church;
that in all they do and say they may stay close to you,
alert to your will and constantly prepared
to move forward where you guide.

Pause

Father, hear us: **keep us in your love.**

We commend to your love
all talks and negotiations in industry
and in matters of international concern;
that they may be marked by generosity of spirit,

and a desire for reconciliation that comes only from you.

Pause

Father, hear us: **keep us in your love.**

We commend to your love
all who are especially precious to us,
and all with whom we find it difficult to relate;
that we may always treat one another
with Christlike love.

Pause

Father, hear us: **keep us in your love.**

We commend to your love all outsiders and outcasts,
all who have been rejected by their family
or their country; that rifts may be healed,
relationships repaired and new bonds of love
forged in Christ.

Pause

Father, hear us: **keep us in your love.**

We commend to your love
those who have reached the end
of their journey on earth;
welcome them into your heavenly kingdom
and bring us, too, at death, safely home.

Heavenly Father, with you beside us our journey is so
richly blessed with joy and peace; how can we ever thank
you for the generosity of your love and ceaseless care!

Merciful Father
**accept these prayers for the sake of your Son,
our Saviour Jesus Christ, Amen.**

Ascension Day and Sunday after Ascension

Jesus has ascended into heaven. With his ministry complete, and death conquered, Jesus takes his place at the right hand of God. No longer tied by time and place he reigns in glory.

Trusting in Christ's victory over all evil,
let us pray to the Father for the world and the Church.

We pray for all who witness to Christ
in spite of danger and persecution;
all who work to bring others to know and love you;
that in your strength they may be blessed,
encouraged and bear much fruit.

Pause

King of glory: **reign in our hearts.**

We pray for those who have never received
the Good News of your saving love;
for those areas where violence and terrorism
make normal life impossible;
that the spirit of Jesus, the Prince of Peace,
may filter through to increase love

and understanding, respect and goodwill.

Pause

King of glory: **reign in our hearts.**

We pray for our families
and those with whom we live and work;
for particular needs known to us personally;
that in everything we do,
and every minute we live,
your name may be glorified and your will be done.

Pause

King of glory: **reign in our hearts.**

We pray for the sick and the dying;
that their trust in you may deepen
until their fears are calmed
and they can look forward with real hope
to meeting their Saviour face to face.

Pause

King of glory: **reign in our hearts.**

We pray for those who have died;
may they wake to the joy of eternal life with you.

We offer you thanks and praise
for your constant love and kindness,
and especially for the joy of your salvation.

Merciful Father
**accept these prayers for the sake of your Son,
our Saviour Jesus Christ, Amen.**

Pentecost

The Holy Spirit is poured out on the disciples
like a rush of wind and with tongues of fire. Ever
since, God's Holy Spirit has enriched and
empowered all who open their hearts and minds
to receive it.

In wonder let us come before the almighty
and everlasting God, to pray in the Spirit of Christ.

We pray for every Christian;
that each may be more receptive to the Holy Spirit,
until every worshipping community is charged
with the vitality and love of the living Christ.

Pause

Loving Father: **let your Spirit live in us now.**

We pray for the world and its leaders;
for its mistakes and tragedies,
misunderstandings and confusion;
may your active Spirit bring
order, serenity and hope.

Pause

Loving Father: **let your Spirit live in us now.**

We pray for a deepening of our own faith,
more understanding of your will,
a clearer awareness of others' needs
and a greater desire to give our lives away.

Pause
Loving Father: **let your Spirit live in us now.**

We pray for those whose lives are darkened by guilt,
resentment or despair;
for those who live violent and cruel lives,
and for all who are ill, injured or abused.

Pause
Loving Father: **let your Spirit live in us now.**

We pray for those who have died in the faith of Christ,
especially...

may they enjoy life with you for ever.

Father, in grateful thanks for all
your blessings in our lives,
we relinquish our wills to yours.

Merciful Father
**accept these prayers
for the sake of your Son,
our Saviour Jesus Christ, Amen.**

Trinity Sunday

The God we worship is Father, Son and Holy Spirit. The qualities of God are revealed in the three persons of the Trinity, and in us, too, when we found our lives on him. Filled with his life, the Christian community will be enabled to show the love of God, the grace of Jesus and the fellowship of the Holy Spirit.

Gathered together in the love and fellowship of God,
let us speak to our Father of our cares and needs.

We pray for the work of your Church
in suburbs, cities, slums and villages all over the world,
especially where there is violent opposition,
complacency or apathy;
that all who work in your name
may be blessed and encouraged,
so many may find peace in your love.

Pause

Abba, Father: **hear your children.**

We pray for the world; for all areas
in which there is a breakdown of communication
between individuals, groups or nations;
may your unifying love draw people together,

helping them to find shared interests to build on,
rather than dwelling on hurtful divisions.

Pause
Abba, Father: **hear your children.**

We pray for a greater love and fellowship amongst us
here in this parish and in our families;
live in us, Father, and make us more ready
to respond and forgive, to help and to listen.

Pause
Abba, Father: **hear your children.**

We pray for the homeless
and those living in crowded, inadequate
accommodation; those living alone and isolated;
for the hungry and malnourished;
may your love, working through us, your body,
reach those in desperate need and give them new hope.

Pause
Abba, Father: **hear your children.**

We pray for those who have travelled through death
to eternity; may they live in your peace
and joy for ever.

Rejoicing in your strength, love and fellowship
we offer you our thanks and praise.

Merciful Father
**accept these prayers for the sake of your Son,
our Saviour Jesus Christ, Amen.**

2nd Sunday after Pentecost
(Trinity 1)

God's people are called to be united in the fellowship of the Spirit, sharing God's life. But we are given free will, so we can choose whether to be part of God's people or not.

Fellow members of the Body of Christ
full of thankfulness for his abiding love
let us pray to our heavenly Father.

Lord, we ask you to deepen
our personal commitment
so that the life-giving sap of the true vine
can flow through the Church and out into the world.

Pause

Live in us, Father: **that we may bear fruit.**

Direct and further all international discussions
so that they lead to peace,
goodwill and mutual understanding.

Pause

Live in us, Father: **that we may bear fruit.**

Lord, come and make your home in us,
in our marriages and our families,
our places of work and our local community;
may our characters be forged by your life within us.

<u>Pause</u>

Live in us, Father: **that we may bear fruit.**

Bring healing and wholeness
to those who are ill;
peace to the anxious,
courage to the fearful
and rest to the weary.

<u>Pause</u>

Live in us, Father: **that we may bear fruit.**

Give everlasting peace
to those who have died in faith;
may they know the joy
of being invited to your heavenly banquet.

We thank you that we are all invited
to share your life-giving love;
make us worthy of all you have promised.

Merciful Father
accept these prayers
for the sake of your Son,
our Saviour Jesus Christ, Amen.

3rd Sunday after Pentecost (Trinity 2)

> Through Christ we die to sin and are raised to full life. Jesus, the Christ, the Son of God, is the fulfilment of the prophecies and the only way to salvation.

Let us pray, my brothers and sisters,
in the knowledge of our Father's infinite mercy.

We pray for all Christian people and Church leaders;
all whose faith is battered through disaster or suffering;
may we know the certainty of your abiding presence
which transforms and rebuilds.

Pause

Touch our lives, Lord: **that we may live.**

We pray for all world leaders,
all administrative bodies and political institutions;
may they be always aware
of the real needs of those they serve
and be effective in providing for them.

Pause

Touch our lives, Lord: **that we may live.**

We pray for our local community,
for our families and our friends,
with all the hopes, fears, problems and needs;
make us ready to serve you
in our own area and spread your life-giving joy.

Pause

Touch our lives, Lord: **that we may live**

We pray for the dying and those
who love and tend them;
for the bereaved and desolate;
may all in trouble and sorrow
draw strength from your life
and your victory over death.

Pause

Touch our lives, Lord: **that we may live.**

We pray for those who have died;
that, falling asleep to this life
they may wake to eternal life
in the joy of heaven.

We thank you, heavenly Father,
for saving us from sin's destruction
and making it possible to live
in such abundant fullness.

Merciful Father,
accept these prayers
for the sake of your Son,
our Saviour Jesus Christ, Amen.

4th Sunday after Pentecost (Trinity 3)

The freedom of the children of God liberates them to serve others. Whenever we deny God through our words or actions it hurts him, because he longs for us to know the freedom and joy of serving him. When we speak and act as his friends there is great joy both for us and in heaven.

My companions in Christ,
let us lay at the feet of our heavenly Father
all our cares and concerns for the Church
and for the world.

We pray for those Christians whom you are calling
to a particular ministry; may they recognise your voice
and respond to it in trust.

Pause

Lord, hear us: **we offer ourselves to your service.**

We pray for all involved with government,
both in our own country and throughout the world;
may the way we govern
reflect the way we are governed by you,

our God of justice, mercy and compassion.

Pause

Lord, hear us: **we offer ourselves to your service.**

We pray that we, and all others worshipping
in this city/town, may allow you access
into more of our life and personality;
so you can work through us
to spread healing and wholeness.

Pause

Lord, hear us: **we offer ourselves to your service.**

We pray for those who have become locked
in their guilt, resentment, self-pity or hatred;
may they be released through thorough repentance
to the joy and freedom of your full forgiveness.

Pause

Lord, hear us: **we offer ourselves to your service.**

We pray for all who have been brought home
to eternity, especially...

may they, through your mercy,
live for ever in your peace.

We offer you grateful thanks and praise
for all this life's blessings which surround us each day;
may we grow in appreciation
and learn to perceive your glory more clearly.

Merciful Father
**accept these prayers for the sake of your Son,
our Saviour Jesus Christ, Amen.**

5th Sunday after Pentecost
(Trinity 4)

God's Law is summed up in love. It is this law
which undergirds us as we work with Christ to
draw all people to the creator, by whom and for
whom we were made.

My sisters and brothers in Christ,
we have been drawn here today by the power
of God's love; into that love let us now gather
all those for whom we pray.

Father, we commend to your love
all who serve you as ministers
of your word and sacrament in the church;
may all they do be an extension of your love.

Pause

Father almighty: **let your will be done.**

Father, we commend to your love
all judges and those serving on juries;
those who make laws in our country
and throughout the world;
may our human laws reflect the unchanging law

and love of your goodness and mercy.

Pause
Father almighty: **let your will be done.**

We commend to your love our own loved ones;
all who will come to our homes this week;
may the welcome they receive
express your welcoming love.

Pause
Father almighty: **let your will be done.**

We commend to your love those whose minds
have been poisoned by exposure to violence;
children who have been abandoned or maltreated;
all who crave affection
but are frightened of getting hurt.

Pause
Father almighty: **let your will be done.**

We commend to your love those
who have died in faith; welcome them
into your kingdom and give them everlasting peace.

We thank you for the privilege of working with you
to spread the Good News of your saving love;
by your grace may we become the kind of people you
intend us to be.

Merciful Father
**accept these prayers for the sake of your Son,
our Saviour Jesus Christ, Amen.**

6th Sunday after Pentecost
(Trinity 5)

In Christ we become a new person. As soon as we turn to approach God, he comes to welcome us; he accepts us just as we are and begins to heal our personalities, increase our capacity to love and to forgive, and enable us to become fully ourselves.

Let us approach our heavenly Father in humility,
as we bring to his restoring love
all our concern for the Church and the world.

Lord, we bring to you
the divided Christian community;
lead us tenderly to wholeness and unity.

Pause

Jesus! Master!: **You alone can make us whole.**

Lord, we bring to you the divided world,
split between wealth and poverty,
complacency and oppression;
break through all barriers
with your love and reconciliation.

Pause

Jesus! Master!: **You alone can make us whole.**

Lord, we bring to you
the wounds and hurts of our own lives;
and of our families;
all unresolved tensions and sorrows,
all reunions, joys and healing;
bless and renew our lives with your living presence.

Pause

Jesus! Master!: **You alone can make us whole.**

Lord, we bring to you all in pain or distress;
the mentally and physically handicapped
and all whom society prefers to ignore;
may your love nourish and heal, accept and restore.

Pause

Jesus! Master!: **You alone can make us whole.**

Lord, we commend to your everlasting
love and care, all who have died, especially ....

With great joy in our hearts
we offer you thanks and praise
for all the gifts and blessings you lavish on us;
may we proclaim our thankfulness by the lives we lead.

Merciful Father
accept these prayers
for the sake of your Son,
our Saviour Jesus Christ, Amen.

7th Sunday after Pentecost (Trinity 6)

Love—the more excellent way of living. God is love, so when we live in love we live in God and he lives in us. In fact, every loving, caring and forgiving act is evidence of God's presence.

My friends in Christ, mindful of God's steadfast love for us let us pray to our heavenly Father.

We pray for faithfulness among all Christians,
particularly when conflicts arise
between Christian values and social expectations;
for a drawing together towards unity
and an increase of the kind of caring
that should make Christ's followers stand out.

Pause

Father, live in us: **fill us with love.**

We pray for all factories, mines, quarries,
all processing and refining plants
and all who work in them or live close by;
may they be safely and responsibly managed
with industrial relations based on

mutual respect, courtesy and goodwill.

Pause
Father, live in us: **fill us with love.**

We pray for everyone who has helped us
and forgiven us this week at home, work or school;
for anyone in need whom we could help;
make us more prepared to take the initiative
in caring for others, and taking ourselves less seriously.

Pause
Father, live in us: **fill us with love.**

We pray for the mal-nourished and starving,
the grief-stricken and the bereaved; for the homeless,
and those surviving in inadequate accommodation;
open our eyes to see Christ among all who suffer,
so we are inspired to spend our lives
in helping those in need.

Pause
Father, live in us: **fill us with love.**

We pray for those who have died;
that falling asleep to pain and suffering
they may wake to the joy and freedom of your heaven.

Lord, your glory is everywhere for us to see, and we
thank you for all the love that brightens our world.

Merciful Father
**accept these prayers for the sake of your Son,
our Saviour Jesus Christ, Amen.**

8th Sunday after Pentecost
(Trinity 7)

What is the fruit of the Spirit? The kind of tree we are will always be shown by the kind of fruit we bear. If we are rooted in Christ, we shall find that our lives blossom and fruit richly.

Led by the Spirit we have come here today.
Trusting in our loving and merciful Father,
let us pray together for the Church and for the world.

We pray for all Christian ministries,
both ordained and lay;
in mutual love may we learn from one another,
grow closer across denominations,
and keep rooted only in Christ.

Pause

Nourish us, Lord: **so that we fruit in joy.**

We pray for all peace initiatives,
all negotiations between nations,
and all attempts at integration;
that, knowing your love for every individual,

we may all respect and honour one another.

Pause
Nourish us, Lord: **so that we fruit in joy.**

We pray for our loved ones – our families
and our friends;
for greater understanding of those
from whom we feel distant;
that we may show your love
in the way we order our relationships.

Pause
Nourish us, Lord: **so that we fruit in joy.**

We pray for those who are far from home;
for those who are exiled or who fear for their lives;
keep them safe,
and help them to know the strength of your presence,
no matter what dangers they face.

Pause
Nourish us, Lord: **so that we fruit in joy.**

We pray that those who have died in faith
may rise in glory, and know your presence for ever.

We thank you for our lovely world
and all the good there is in it;
may we be as generous as you are.

Merciful Father
**accept these prayers for the sake of your Son,
our Saviour Jesus Christ, Amen.**

9th Sunday after Pentecost (Trinity 8)

Putting on the whole armour of God. On our own we are not powerful enough to fight against evil, but God's power of goodness is sufficient for any evil we may meet, and he promises to give us that power when we put ourselves into his care.

Companions in Christ,
knowing that our heavenly Father has sufficient grace
for all our needs, let us pray to him now.

Lord, we pray for the leaders and ministers
of your Church, especially those for whom
your work has brought danger and persecution;
may they never lose sight of your presence,
which comforts and protects.

Pause

Lord of power: **deliver us from evil.**

We pray for clear light and guidance as our world faces
the problems and crises of another week;
for the willingness of leaders

to be wisely advised and courageous
in doing what is right.

Pause

Lord of power: **deliver us from evil.**

We pray for a greater willingness in us
to live and work in your strength;
for a deepening trust in your power
to save, heal and overcome temptation.

Pause

Lord of power: **deliver us from evil.**

We pray for all addicted to drugs,
alcohol, solvent abuse, violence,
or any other habit that enslaves;
for all victims of war, and abuse;
for the terrified and the suicidal.

Pause

Lord of power: **deliver us from evil.**

We pray that all who have passed from this life
may live in the joy of your presence for ever.

Thank you, Father, for all the evils
that have been conquered,
and all the good that is done through your power
every day throughout our world.
Help us to notice your goodness.

Merciful Father
**accept these prayersfor the sake of your Son,
our Saviour Jesus Christ, Amen.**

10th Sunday after Pentecost (Trinity 9)

Reflecting on the nature of Christ. It is, perhaps, his amazing humility which touches us most. For although he understands all things, not only on earth but in the entire universe, and although he is fully in charge, he was prepared to live and die among created beings in order to save them. He, the Lord, serves his people.

We are all brothers and sisters in Christ;
as children of God, our heavenly Father,
let us draw near and tell him of our needs and cares,
asking for his help and blessing.

We ask you, Lord, to bless and guide all who serve you;
to inspire their teaching,
nudge their memories, instruct them
through their failures and mature them
through their experiences,
so that in all activity, your will may be done.

Pause

Merciful Lord: **work on us till we shine with love.**

We ask you to direct the people of the world
towards harmony and peace,
mutual respect and appreciation

of one another's cultures and traditions;
make us prepared to learn from one another.

Pause

Merciful Lord: **work on us till we shine with love.**

We ask you into our homes and places of work,
so that all our friendships, and business transactions,
shopping and leisure times may be opportunities
for rejoicing in your love and spreading your peace.

Pause

Merciful Lord: **work on us till we shine with love.**

We ask you to ease the burdens
of those bowed down by grief, depression,
pain or guilt; encourage the timid and frightened,
refresh all who are overworked
or who have not been able to sleep;
break down all barricades of hatred and revenge.

Pause

Merciful Lord: **work on us till we shine with love.**

We ask you to welcome into your kingdom
all who have died in faith;
may they live for ever in your perfect peace.

Every day we are given so many blessings;
we offer you our thanks and life-long praise.

Merciful Father
**accept these prayers for the sake of your Son,
our Saviour Jesus Christ, Amen.**

11th Sunday after Pentecost
(Trinity 10)

> The serving community. Our belief in Jesus as the Son of God is bound to lead on to serving the world as he did. Through our loving and unflinching service we proclaim to the world the generous, caring nature of God.

Companions in Christ, in confidence
let us pray to our heavenly Father.

We pray that all baptised Christians
may pray without ceasing
and work enthusiastically
to serve the world with love and sensitivity.

Pause

Almighty Father: **may we shine with your light.**

We pray that all disputes and misunderstandings
may be brought to a settled peace,
based on mutual respect, honour,
and a concern for each other's grievances.

Pause

Almighty Father: **may we shine with your light.**

We pray that every home in this parish
may be enfolded in your love,
brightened by your joy
and calmed by your unbroken peace.

Pause
Almighty Father: **may we shine with your light.**

We pray that any who are in great pain
may be granted relief and comfort;
that all who live in constant fear or distress
may be granted a real assurance
of your undergirding and full protection.

Pause
Almighty Father: **may we shine with your light.**

We pray that all who have died may,
through your mercy,
rest in your peace.

We thank you for all your blessings
and especially for the example of Jesus,
in whose strength we offer ourselves for your service.

Merciful Father
**accept these prayers
for the sake of your Son,
our Saviour Jesus Christ, Amen.**

12th Sunday after Pentecost
(Trinity 11)

The Church as a witnessing community. Since we are the members of Christ's body, it is our witness and example that will either repel or draw others to seek God's face. Unless we display Christ's love, many will never see it.

My friends in Christ, let us pray to our heavenly Father trusting in his generous mercy.

We pray for the church as it witnesses
to Christ in the world;
may its members be always aware
that they are called to be servants,
ready and happy to minister to the spiritual, emotional
and physical needs of all people.

Pause

Lord of light: **shine through our lives.**

We pray for the leaders of every community and nation;
may governments reflect the values
of responsible caring, compassion and integrity,

so that no individual or minority group
is abused or left in need.

Pause

Lord of light: **shine through our lives.**

We pray for a breaking down of any complacency
or blindness in us
until we are able to see the needs around us,
and can work in your strength,
giving our whole lives away
in loving those whom you love.

Pause

Lord of light: **shine through our lives.**

We pray for the rejected, neglected,
shunned or despised;
for the unwanted and the disturbed;
for the ill and the injured;
may they be healed, restored and comforted.

Pause

Lord of light: **shine through our lives.**

We pray for those who have passed
through the gateway of death into eternity;
may they know the joy of your presence for ever.

We offer you our thanks
for every opportunity we are given
to witness to your unfailing love; may our words and
our lives proclaim your glory.

Merciful Father
**accept these prayers for the sake of your Son,
our Saviour Jesus Christ, Amen.**

13th Sunday after Pentecost (Trinity 12)

Just as Christ suffered, so we also will suffer. But the suffering is not negative and demoralising; it is even cause for rejoicing, because through the crucifixion and death of Christ came the resurrection. As we share his suffering we shall also share his glorious life.

My sisters and brothers in Christ,
let us bring to the Lord of life
our concern and care for the Church
and for the world.

Lord, we bring before you all Christians,
especially church leaders and pastors;
may they remain faithful in times of trial,
trusting in your everlasting love;
may all who take risks to witness
be given courage and inspiration.

Pause

Lord, in mercy: **hear our cry.**

We bring before you
all the diverse societies of our world;
may your living Spirit be spread

to purify the corrupt, inspire the apathetic
and unlock the hearts of the bigoted.

Pause

Lord, in mercy: **hear our cry.**

We bring before you our own circle of family
and friends; all our desires and attempts to follow you;
live within us to protect, guide,
and bring us to perfection in Christ.

Pause

Lord, in mercy: **hear our cry.**

We bring before you the weak and the frightened;
all who are suffering in any way;
may they find you there with them,
and draw hope and courage from your presence.

Pause

Lord, in mercy: **hear our cry.**

We bring before you those who have died in faith;
may they know the joy and peace
of your heaven for ever.

We thank you and praise you
for all you were prepared to suffer for us;
bring the light of resurrection to all our suffering,
until we learn to praise you even through dark times.

Merciful Father
**accept these prayers for the sake of your Son,
our Saviour Jesus Christ, Amen.**

14th Sunday after Pentecost (Trinity 13)

The family. God loves and cares for us, his children, with parental love, and we are a spiritual family, with Christ our brother. Our own relationships should reflect this strong bond of love and affection; the kind of love which is not possessive but liberating.

My brothers and sisters in Christ,
let us come before God our Father
with our burdens, cares and joys.

Father, bless our Christian family,
both in this parish and throughout the world;
may we witness to your love by the kind of lives
we lead and the work we do in your name.

Pause

Father, live among us: **keep us in your love.**

Bless and guide the leaders of each country
and each community; may we not wander
as sheep without a shepherd but rather be led
and directed by you in the path of peace.

Pause

Father, live among us: **keep us in your love.**

Father, bless our own homes
and our relationships with our parents,
marriage partners, brothers, sisters and children;
may we learn to see and experience
Christ in one another, and cheerfully love
and serve with generosity of spirit.

Pause

Father, live among us: **keep us in your love.**

Bless and protect all families at risk
from evil and danger, either within or without;
for children born with brain damage or deformity
and for their families; for marriages
which are strained and difficult;
that wherever much is demanded,
much strength and support may be given.

Pause

Father, live among us: **keep us in your love.**

Welcome into your kingdom, Father,
all your children who have died, especially...

may we one day share the joy and peace
of coming home to you for ever.

We thank you for the everyday blessings
and fun of family life; both in our own
and in our spiritual family.

Merciful Father
**accept these prayers for the sake of your Son,
our Saviour Jesus Christ, Amen.**

15th Sunday after Pentecost (Trinity 14)

Those in authority. All authority stems from God, and when temporal leaders remember this, good government results. Corruption in authority begins when God's supremity is ignored, rejected or usurped. For us, as citizens of heaven through God's grace, loyalty to God's kingdom must always come first; that may well be shown by our loyalty to others in authority.

Our heavenly Father assures us that
wherever two or three meet in his name
he will be with them; in confidence, then,
let us bring him our needs and cares.

We pray that your love will spill out
through your Church to the world,
filling all teaching, all advice and counsel,
all authority and correction.

Pause

We are your people: **hear us, Lord, we pray.**

May your spirit of forgiveness and justice
permeate the social and political fabric of our world,
till we are able to rule wisely, discuss differences calmly

and be prepared to negotiate rationally.

Pause

We are your people: **hear us, Lord, we pray.**

May your light shine in our hearts
to show us our faults and enable us to admit them;
to shine through our lives
in the way we treat one another,
especially when we disagree or feel hurt.

Pause

We are your people: **hear us, Lord, we pray.**

May your comfort and consolation
soothe those who are afraid or in great pain,
refresh those who are mentally or physically exhausted
and be a life line to those who are broken hearted
or in despair.

Pause

We are your people: **hear us, Lord, we pray.**

May those who have passed into eternity
be welcomed into your heavenly kingdom
to live with you for ever.

We praise you, Lord,
for all the joy and gladness of our lives;
for the beauty of your world
and the affection of our loved ones.

Merciful Father
**accept these prayers for the sake of your Son,
our Saviour Jesus Christ, Amen.**

16th Sunday after Pentecost
(Trinity 15)

Loving our neighbour. Since God made all of us—even those we may not like or whose behaviour we may disapprove of—we are to love one another and help those in need, regardless of whether they are friends of ours or not.

My companions in Christ,
humbled by the wonder of God's love for us all,
let us lay before him our needs and concerns.

We lay before you all Christians, especially
Church leaders, bishops and all in ordained ministry;
Christians who have lapsed from worshipping
or whose prayer life is dead;
may all be touched and strengthened
by your caring love.

Pause

Father of all: **increase our love for one another.**

We lay before you the heated arguments,
industrial action, blinkered vision
and stubborn behaviour of our world;
may the power of your love soften, ease and coax us all

to be more understanding, wise and forgiving.

Pause
Father of all: **increase our love for one another.**

We lay before you the areas of our own lives
which are in shadow and darkness; that in the light
of your love we may see our faults and weaknesses
more clearly, notice the good in those we live with,
and recognise the needs around us.

Pause
Father of all: **increase our love for one another.**

We lay before you widows, widowers and orphans,
all broken families and all the lonely; the disfigured,
incapacitated and neglected; those who daily persevere
in tending a physically or mentally sick relative;
may the warmth and joy of your love
comfort and transform.

Pause
Father of all: **increase our love for one another.**

We commend to your keeping all those who have died;
may they rest in your peace.

We thank you for all the blessings
which enrich our lives; for the opportunities to show
our praise in loving service to one another.

Merciful Father
**accept these prayers for the sake of your Son,
our Saviour Jesus Christ, Amen.**

17th Sunday after Pentecost (Trinity 16)

The kind of life we lead proclaims the kind of faith we have. We may say we believe in God, but that is only true if we live a life compatible with belief in the God of love. It will be our kindness, thoughtfulness, self-control and generosity which best prove our faith real.

In the Spirit of Christ and taught by his example,
let us pray trustingly to our heavenly Father.

We pray for Christian witnesses throughout the world,
with all their weaknesses, gifts,
victories and disappointments;
May all Christians reflect your brilliant light
to direct others to worship you
and experience the joy of your peace.

Pause

Lord, we believe: **help our unbelief.**

We pray for all inhabitants of our planet
in the daily routines, the work and leisure;
for the silent majorities and all elected to govern;
may all leaders truly represent the needs of their

people, and may we live in peace with one another.

Pause

Lord, we believe: **help our unbelief.**

We pray for our loved ones;
for friends with whom we have lost touch;
for any we have let down; and for ourselves;
may the Spirit we have been so privileged to receive
burn more brightly in our lives.

Pause

Lord, we believe: **help our unbelief.**

We pray for all who are undergoing
long-term or chronic illness,
slow recovery or mental anguish
with no end or hope in sight;
may they hold on to you,
receiving your strength and love
and knowing that in you they are safe.

Pause

Lord, we believe: **help our unbelief.**

We pray that those who have died
may rise to eternal life in you, and that at our death,
we too may share your peace for ever.

We offer you all our thanks and praise
for your generous love and kindness to all your people;
may we show our praise in our generosity to others.

Merciful Father
**accept these prayers for the sake of your Son,
our Saviour Jesus Christ, Amen.**

18th Sunday after Pentecost
(Trinity 17)

Offering our lives to God's service. God has given us so much that our thankfulness prompts us to show our love in acts of generosity, both to God in worship, and to one another wherever there is need.

Brothers and sisters in Christ,
in the knowledge of God's love for us
let us pray for the Church and for the world.

We pray for all clergy serving
in deprived or violent areas of the world;
all who are in personal danger for teaching the faith;
may they be reassured and their service blessed
by the power of your love.

Pause

Abba, Father: **we belong to you.**

We pray for all who serve in
positions of authority in this country
and throughout the world;
for all debates and international talks;
may the power of reason you have given us

lead us towards your truth and wisdom.

Pause

Abba, Father: **we belong to you.**

We pray for those we serve each day,
and those who serve us;
for relationships we find difficult,
and for situations which tend to make us irritable;
increase our generosity of spirit,
and our delight in serving others.

Pause

Abba, Father: **we belong to you.**

We pray for the resentful,
and all who suffer injustice or neglect;
for all in need from natural disasters,
war, famine or disease;
may your love reach them through our care.

Pause

Abba, Father: **we belong to you.**

We pray that all who have died in faith
may know the joy of heaven for ever.

We rejoice in all the goodness and generosity
your love has inspired in so many people;
for the way you encourage and guide us.

Merciful Father
**accept these prayers for the sake of your Son,
our Saviour Jesus Christ, Amen.**

19th Sunday after Pentecost (Trinity 18)

Living by faith. Faith is what gives us hope and certainty about things we can't actually see. It enables us to step out confidently into the future, and it gives us courage in the face of threats and danger.

In the Spirit of Jesus Christ, our brother,
let us draw near to our heavenly Father
and pray to him together.

We pray for all who labour in the painstaking work
of building up the kingdom of heaven;
guide them in uncertainty,
encourage them in apparent failure,
and train them in trust through perseverance.

Pause

Father of great mercy: **we trust you to help us.**

We pray for the leaders of our country
and of all peoples throughout the world;
for newspaper editors, film directors
and all who influence our nation through the media;

may our world be led to understand your values,
and know your peace.

Pause
Father of great mercy: **we trust you to help us.**

We pray for those we rely on and those who rely on us;
for an increase of loyalty and trust;
for guidance in the way we use
our time, money and abilities;
for courage to commit our lives to you more deeply.

Pause
Father of great mercy: **we trust you to help us.**

We pray for those who have lost their way in life,
and long to be rescued and loved back to wholeness;
for those suffering through illness
or handicap or accident.

Pause
Father of great mercy: **we trust you to help us.**

We pray for those who have passed
through the gateway of death into eternity;
may they abide in your peace for ever.

We thank you for the many blessings of life
which you give us each day;
for the wonder of your creation
and the joy and comfort of your presence.

Merciful Father
**accept these prayers for the sake of your Son,
our Saviour Jesus Christ, Amen.**

20th Sunday after Pentecost (Trinity 19)

Steadfast endurance. By his own example and encouragement, Jesus inspires us to continue faithful even through the difficult and rough passages of life; in fact, it is often through such perseverance that we are enabled to mature spiritually, and grow to fulfill our potential.

Fellow members of Christ, we have been drawn here,
united in his love; let us pray together,
confident in God's faithfulness.

We pray for every newly baptised Christian;
for all recently confirmed and ordained;
may they be strengthened and encouraged
to witness faithfully and bravely,
strong in your strength.

Pause

Give us courage, Lord: **to do your will.**

We pray for our world,
so richly blessed and so full of potential;
give us the grace to persevere in what is right,

to use the world's resources for good.

Pause
Give us courage, Lord: **to do your will.**

We pray for all of us here,
for our families and our friends;
inspire us to work at our relationships
and remind us to welcome you
into every situation we meet.

Pause
Give us courage, Lord: **to do your will.**

We pray for those whose bodies or minds
are weak and diseased;
for those too ill or exhausted to pray;
for all who nurse and care
for the chronically or terminally ill.

Pause
Give us courage, Lord: **to do your will.**

We pray for the bereaved and those who have died;
may they wake to the eternal joy of your heaven.

We give you our thanks and praise
for your steadfast love
which gives us strength and courage.

Merciful Father
accept these prayers
for the sake of your Son,
our Saviour Jesus Christ, Amen.

21st Sunday after Pentecost (Trinity 20)

Christian hope. As adopted children of God, we know that this world and this life is not the whole story. We are children of eternity, living in the faith that this life does not finish at death, and our true spiritual home is in heaven, towards which we are walking as joyful pilgrims.

As sons and daughters of our heavenly Father,
let us pray together, trusting in his love.

We pray that the Church and all its members
may not be stagnant, but flow forward
in the direction you want it to go;
may the Christian hope burn brightly
in our lives and may your kingdom come.

Pause

Lord, you are our hope: **we believe and trust in you.**

We pray that we may all tend and care
for the world you have given us to live in;
may we share its food and riches,

and use them wisely and safely
without waste or destruction.

Pause

Lord, you are our hope: **we believe and trust in you.**

We pray for the sick, the injured and the distressed;
for the dying and for those who mourn;
may your healing presence
bring wholeness and comfort.

Pause

Lord, you are our hope: **we believe and trust in you.**

We pray for our own circle of family and friends;
for personal spiritual growth;
may we be more watchful,
preparing ourselves more thoroughly
day by day to meet you face to face.

Pause

Lord, you are our hope: **we believe and trust in you.**

We pray for those who have died in faith
and live with you in glory;
may we one day share with them
the joy of being in your presence for ever.

We thank you, Father,
for all your goodness and kindness to us;
for the hope of heaven and the comfort of your love.

Merciful Father
**accept these prayers for the sake of your Son,
our Saviour Jesus Christ, Amen.**

22nd Sunday after Pentecost (Trinity 21)

We cannot serve two masters—if we choose to serve God we shall not be able to continue as slaves of money and materialism. We should be as astute about our spiritual lives as the dishonest steward was about keeping his job.

My companions in Christ,
having promised to commit our lives to God,
let us pray to him now.

We pray that all Christians
may stay true to their calling;
may they witness to the value
of caring, selfless love, and draw others
to acknowledge you as Lord.

Pause

Lord, take us: **help us to live.**

We pray for all monarchs, presidents
and those in positions of power;
for those whom they rule,
and those with whom they negotiate;

that peace and justice may prevail over all our earth.

Pause

Lord take us: **help us to live.**

We pray for ourselves, our families,
friends and neighbours;
may we acknowledge
our failings as well as our strengths,
and serve you in serving one another.

Pause

Lord take us: **help us to live.**

We pray for the poor, the weak and the oppressed;
for the abandoned, neglected and abused;
may all obstacles to their healing
and wholeness be removed,
through the outpouring of your love and hope.

Pause

Lord, take us: **help us to live.**

We pray for those who have died;
may they know the eternal joy
of living in your presence for ever.

We thank you for the fresh joys
and challenges of each day;
for the love and encouragement your Spirit gives us.

Merciful Father,
**accept these prayers for the sake of your Son,
our Saviour Jesus Christ, Amen.**

Last Sunday after Pentecost

We are citizens of heaven, gradually making our way home. Before anything was created, and after the end of time, our God continues to reign. All who love him have been promised a share in his Kingdom of heaven.

As sons and daughters of our heavenly King
let us ask our Father's blessing
on the Church and on the world.

We pray for the work of Christ's body, the Church;
that all may labour zealously
for the establishment of your Kingdom on earth;
till the world is flooded
with your peace, joy and love.

Pause

Lord, our heavenly Father: **may your kingdom come.**

We pray for the work of all peacemakers,
all who work for justice, reconciliation and harmony;

that you, Lord God of peace and love,
will bless, support and encourage them.

Pause

Lord, our heavenly Father: **may your kingdom come.**

We pray for our own work in this life;
that we may dedicate our energies and resources
more fully to your will, undertaking every task
and activity joyfully, trusting in your strength.

Pause

Lord, our heavenly Father: **may your kingdom come.**

We pray for the work of those who heal
and tend the sick, the injured and the dying;
for all in their care;
for all involved in medical research
and those whose lives depend on drugs,
dialysis or chemotherapy.

Pause

Lord, our heavenly Father: **may your kingdom come.**

We pray for all who have passed
through the gate of death to eternity;
may they live for ever in your heaven.

We rejoice for all the wonder and beauty
of your creation; in the constant miracle
of life and renewal; in your amazing
and undeserved love and affection for us.

Merciful Father
**accept these prayers for the sake of your Son,
our Saviour Jesus Christ, Amen.**